TRANSFORMING LIVES

EMPOWERING SENIORS TO LIVE THEIR DREAMS

HELEN CUMMINGS-HENRY

The
Transformation Lady

Contents

Introduction

Hello Beautiful People and Welcome to a chapter of life that defies all boundaries—the senior years. This is not a book about slowing down; it's a vibrant celebration of stepping into an era where limitations are mere illusions and possibilities are boundless.

Think about it: every passing year isn't just a number; it's a mosaic of experiences, lessons, and adventures that have shaped who you are today. Now, you're on the cusp of a new chapter, and trust me, it's anything but ordinary.

Here, within these pages, you won't find advice on settling down or taking it easy. Instead, you'll uncover a treasure trove of ideas, inspirations, and opportunities waiting for you to seize. This isn't the time for sitting idly by; it's the time to leap into uncharted territories, to chase dreams, and to redefine what it means to truly live.

The senior years aren't an epilogue; they're an exhilarating prologue to a narrative waiting to be written—one brimming with vitality, wisdom, and the uncontainable spirit of someone who knows that the best is yet to come.

The passage of time leads us down varied paths, each phase of life offering unique lessons, challenges, and opportunities. As the years accumulate and the calendar pages turn, there comes a significant juncture: the entry into the senior years.

This phase, often characterized by societal perceptions of winding down, holds far more significance than merely the count of years lived. It embodies a chapter of renewal, transformation, and newfound purpose. This chapter aims to delve into the essence of embracing the senior years—a time not of limitations but of possibilities, not of stagnation but of growth.

The transition into the senior years is an evolution that demands a profound shift in mindset. It beckons the individual to discard preconceived notions of age-bound restrictions and instead embrace this phase as an era ripe with opportunities for reinvention and self-discovery. It's a pivotal moment to redefine success, moving away from traditional metrics and embracing a more holistic definition that intertwines personal fulfillment with the richness of experiences and relationships.

Within this transition, retirement stands as a hallmark—a milestone often marked by both liberation and emotional intricacies. It's more than a cessation of professional duties; it marks a shift in roles and responsibilities, demanding an exploration of identity beyond the confines of a career. As the curtain falls on one chapter, it opens the door to a canvas waiting to be painted with the vibrant hues of newfound passions and untapped potentials.

The chapters ahead delve into the nuances of this transition, exploring the emotional landscapes, redefining success, and uncovering the beauty in embracing change. The senior years beckon not as a conclusion but as a prologue to a new narrative—a tale of resilience, growth, and the enduring pursuit of a life enriched by purpose, wisdom, and the relentless quest for fulfillment.

So, are you ready to embrace the remarkable, to live boldly, and to discover the myriad of adventures that await you in this extraordinary phase of life? If the answer is yes, then turn the page and let's begin this remarkable journey together.

Embracing Your Senior Years

Welcome to a life teeming with boundless possibilities. Here, we embark on a journey that redefines aging not as a period of decline, but as an extraordinary phase ripe with opportunities for growth, joy, and fulfillment.

We'll explore the art of embracing this remarkable stage of life with open arms, exuding positivity, and radiating enthusiasm. We'll uncover the profound impact of staying mentally agile, physically vibrant, and socially engaged as well as spiritually connected.

So, let's dive into the vibrant tapestry of the senior years, where every day is an invitation to embrace life's wonders and relish the infinite prospects that await.

The Transition into Senior Years

Entering the senior years marks a new phase of life, one that offers unique opportunities for growth, fulfillment, and joy. This chapter focuses on the significance of embracing this phase with a positive outlook and the vitality to lead a purposeful life.

The senior years herald a profound shift in perspective—a juncture where the notion of productivity evolves from career achievements to personal fulfillment. Embracing this change entails redefining success and finding value in experiences, relationships, and newfound freedoms. It's about transcending the societal narrative that associates aging with limitations, and instead, embracing it as an opportunity for renewed purpose and exploration.

Marie, at 68, found herself at a crossroads upon retiring from her lifelong career as a teacher. While her colleagues settled into a quieter life, she decided to embrace this new chapter with vigor. Instead of seeing retirement as an end, she viewed it as a beginning—a chance to explore uncharted territories.

She joined community classes, delving into subjects she'd always been curious about but never had the time to explore. From pottery to history classes, each day brought new discoveries. This mental stimulation invigorated her spirit, keeping her mind sharp and her enthusiasm for learning alive.

However, Marie didn't limit her activities to solitary pursuits. She recognized the vitality of social engagement. Volunteering at a local library allowed her to connect with others, sharing her love for books while forging new friendships. From book clubs to community events, her social circle blossomed, enriching her life in ways she hadn't anticipated.

Marie's radiant enthusiasm for life became infectious. Her positivity and zest for learning didn't just inspire fellow seniors; it became a beacon of hope for those entering their golden years. She embodied the essence of embracing later years with an open heart, demonstrating that age wasn't a hindrance but a canvas awaiting colorful strokes of new experiences and connections.

Understanding Transitions

The transition into retirement is more than a logistical adjustment; it's an emotional journey marked by the ebb and flow of expectations. Retiring often entails bidding farewell to a structured routine, a career that once defined identity, and a network of colleagues. It can evoke feelings of liberation and loss simultaneously. Understanding this emotional rollercoaster and acknowledging the complex web of emotions—excitement, nostalgia, uncertainty—forms the first step toward navigating this transition with grace and resilience.

As roles and responsibilities shift, there's a chance to reassess one's identity outside the confines of a job title. The newfound freedom may initially feel overwhelming, but it offers a canvas to paint a different picture of fulfillment—one drawn from personal passions, unexplored hobbies, and connections that were previously put on hold. It's a phase ripe with possibilities, demanding a recalibration of goals and a reevaluation of what constitutes a meaningful life.

Transitioning into the senior years demands an open-minded approach, allowing room for the unexpected, and a willingness to embrace change. It's a pivot from the hustle of professional life to a more serene pace, offering opportunities to delve into pursuits long put aside. This transition is not just about the end of a chapter but the beginning of a new narrative—one enriched by experiences, wisdom, and the freedom to craft a life aligned with personal aspirations.

Positivity and Well-being

The foundation of positive aging lies in cultivating a mindset that transcends the stereotypes often associated with growing older. It's a recognition that a positive outlook isn't merely a choice but a cornerstone for overall well-being and longevity. Research affirms the profound impact of optimism on mental and physical health, demonstrating that a positive mindset can reduce stress, enhance immune function, and even increase lifespan. Embracing positivity isn't denying life's challenges; rather, it's about navigating them with resilience and hope.

Thomas, an 72-year-old retired engineer, approached his senior years with a determination to stay physically active. He didn't perceive age as a barrier but as an incentive to maintain his vitality. Instead of slowing down, he joined a dance class—a hobby he'd always been intrigued by but never explored.

Initially hesitant, he found himself immersed in the rhythms of dance. The physical movement not only kept him active but also invigorated his spirit. From salsa to ballroom, he discovered the joy of movement, which not only helped him stay physically fit but also brought immense joy and camaraderie.

Thomas didn't limit his activities to the dance floor; he recognized the importance of mental agility too. He joined discussion groups, engaging in debates and book clubs that kept his mind stimulated. The combination of physical activity and mental engagement filled his days with vibrancy and purpose.

His commitment to an active lifestyle sent ripples through his community. His contagious enthusiasm for dance and learning became an inspiration. Thomas demonstrated that staying active wasn't confined to a gym or classroom but was an attitude—a zest for life that infused each day with vitality and joy.

Resilience in Aging

Seniors exemplify resilience—an invaluable asset that helps navigate the twists and turns that life presents. In the face of changes, loss, or health challenges, resilience stands as a guiding force, empowering individuals to adapt and thrive. It's not about avoiding difficulties but rather about bouncing back stronger, fostering a sense of empowerment and strength. Resilience in aging isn't a trait reserved for the select few; it's a skill that can be honed, allowing seniors to weather storms and emerge with newfound wisdom and fortitude.

As the sands of time continue to shift, the power of positive aging becomes increasingly evident. It's a recognition that age doesn't diminish the capacity for joy, growth, or contribution. Seniors embracing positivity often find themselves more equipped to tackle life's hurdles, armed with a mindset that not only sustains but propels them toward greater fulfillment and contentment.

Positivity isn't a passive state but an active choice—an intentional lens through which seniors view their experiences. It's a perspective that allows them to extract meaning from life's moments, savoring the richness of relationships, discoveries, and personal growth.

Staying Active: Mind, Body, and Socially

Engaging actively in various dimensions of life remains pivotal for seniors to lead fulfilling and vibrant lives. Staying active isn't solely about physical exertion; it encompasses mental stimulation, physical fitness, and social engagement. This trifecta forms the cornerstone of a holistic approach to wellness in the senior years.

Mental Stimulation

Keeping the mind agile and curious is as crucial as maintaining physical health. Mental activities like puzzles, learning new skills, or engaging in stimulating conversations help seniors preserve cognitive function and prevent mental decline. The pursuit of lifelong learning or hobbies sparks neurons, fostering mental resilience and creativity.

Physical Health

Physical activity isn't reserved for the young; it's a vital component of healthy aging. Tailored exercises for seniors, including walking, yoga, or light strength training, contribute to improved balance, flexibility, and overall well-being. It's about adapting workouts to individual needs, focusing on maintaining mobility and preventing injuries, enhancing not just physical health but also mental and emotional balance.

Social Engagement

The richness of life often resides in meaningful connections. Social interaction among seniors promotes a sense of belonging, reduces feelings of isolation, and bolsters emotional well-being. Engaging in community activities, clubs, or volunteering opportunities provides avenues for socializing, sharing experiences, and nurturing friendships, contributing significantly to a fulfilling life.

The integration of these elements, mental, physical, and social, forms a holistic approach to active aging. It's a proactive stance that empowers seniors to lead purposeful lives, ensuring that each day is filled with mental vitality, physical vitality, and a robust social network that nurtures their spirits.

Rediscovering Purpose

The later years aren't an endpoint but a new chapter ripe with opportunities to explore uncharted territories of purpose and passion. Seniors often find immense fulfillment by delving into activities that ignite their spirits—be it learning a new craft, pursuing an artistic endeavor, or engaging in volunteer work. These endeavors not only infuse life with newfound enthusiasm but also grant a sense of purpose that revitalizes each day with meaning and fulfillment.

Legacy Building

Reflecting on a life lived is an art seniors excel at. Their experiences, wisdom, and stories carry invaluable lessons that, when shared, transcend time. Legacy building isn't just about material bequests; it's about imparting knowledge, values, and life lessons to future generations. Seniors have the unique opportunity to weave a legacy that resonates with their life's journey, ensuring that their contributions endure, enriching the lives of those who come after them.

In the canvas of later years, purpose isn't a static entity but a dynamic force that evolves and adapts. It's about discovering or rediscovering passions that invigorate the soul, bringing joy and fulfillment. The pursuit of purpose isn't constrained by age; rather, it thrives in the wisdom, experiences, and untapped potential accumulated over a lifetime.

Building a legacy isn't solely about leaving a mark but about fostering a continuous ripple effect. It's about passing on not just possessions but the intangible gifts of wisdom, resilience, and values that shape future generations. Seniors embody a wealth of experiences that, when shared, become guiding lights for those who follow, imparting a legacy of immeasurable worth.

Embracing the senior years is not merely about counting the years but about making the years count. It's a time to savor life's experiences, nurture relationships, and continue to grow. By staying active mentally, physically, and socially, seniors can navigate this chapter of life with enthusiasm and a sense of fulfillment. This chapter aims to inspire a proactive approach to aging and encourage seniors to embrace this stage of life as an opportunity for new adventures and personal growth.

Questions to Explore: Embracing Your Senior Years

1. **Positivity and Attitude:**

   - How will maintaining a positive attitude benefit in navigating the challenges and opportunities that come with aging?

   - Can you share personal experiences or examples of how a positive mindset has influenced your approach to later years?

2. **Mental Stimulation and Engagement:**

   - What are some effective ways for you to keep your mind active and engaged?

   - How does mental stimulation contribute to a sense of fulfillment and purpose in later life?

3. **Physical Activity and Well-being:**

   - Why is it crucial for you to maintain physical activity? What are the benefits beyond just physical health?

   - What are some practical and enjoyable ways for you to incorporate physical activities into their daily routines?

4. **Social Interaction and Community Engagement:**

   - How does social interaction impact your overall well-being?

- What strategies or activities do you use to encourage social engagement, especially for those who may feel isolated?

5. **Challenges and Resilience:**

    - What are some common challenges that you face when trying to stay active mentally, physically, and socially, and how can you overcome these challenges?

    - How does cultivating resilience play a role in embracing the later years with enthusiasm and staying active across different aspects of life?

CHAPTER ONE SUMMARY

In the inaugural chapter, "Embracing Your Senior Years," the focus is on empowering seniors to view their later years as a period ripe with opportunities for personal growth and fulfillment. The narrative emphasizes the vital importance of approaching this phase of life with a positive mindset and a zest for new experiences.

Throughout the chapter, the significance of remaining active in various facets of life is underscored. Seniors are encouraged to engage mentally, physically, and socially, recognizing these as pillars of a fulfilling life in the later years. Mental stimulation through continued learning, embracing new hobbies, or pursuing lifelong passions is highlighted as a means to keep the mind sharp and engaged.

The chapter places a strong emphasis on the importance of physical activity for seniors. It outlines various exercises and activities tailored to their needs, promoting a healthy lifestyle that contributes to their overall well-being. Additionally, the narrative stresses the value of maintaining an active social life, nurturing relationships, and actively participating in community engagements, all of which are pivotal in fostering a sense of belonging and purpose.

Overall, "Embracing Your Senior Years" serves as a foundational guide, advocating for a proactive and optimistic approach to aging. It serves as a source of inspiration and guidance for seniors, encouraging them to embrace this stage of life with enthusiasm while providing actionable insights to lead a vibrant and fulfilling lifestyle.

CHAPTER 2

SETTING AND PURSUING DREAMS

Exploring Dreams and Aspirations

Dreams are the heartbeat of the human spirit, transcending age and time. They embody aspirations, desires, and ambitions, serving as guiding stars that light the path toward personal fulfillment. Regardless of age, the pursuit of dreams remains a fundamental aspect of human existence, reminding us that the possibilities for growth and achievement are limitless.

Stories of Seniors Pursuing Dreams

The tales of seniors who dared to pursue their dreams after retirement are a testament to the unwavering spirit that defies the boundaries of age. These narratives echo resilience, determination, and a refusal to let the sands of time dampen the fire within. They serve as inspiring examples of individuals who refused to be confined by societal expectations, embracing their passions wholeheartedly and carving out new avenues for personal achievement and satisfaction.

The Artistic Awakening

Eleanor, at 70, discovered her lifelong passion for painting after retiring from her administrative career. Though she had dabbled in art during her younger days, the demands of work had kept her passion on the back burner. However, retirement presented an opportunity to reignite her artistic flame.

Investing in art supplies and enrolling in painting classes, Eleanor found solace and joy in bringing canvases to life. Her paintings reflected her newfound freedom—bold strokes capturing landscapes and emotions. With each stroke, she rediscovered a part of herself that had been dormant for years. Soon, her artworks adorned local galleries, and her passion transformed into a source of pride and fulfillment.

The Traveling Duo

John and Margaret, both in their late 60s, had harbored dreams of exploring the world together. Retirement finally granted them the freedom to pursue their shared aspiration of globetrotting. Armed with backpacks and an adventurous spirit, they embarked on a journey to visit destinations they had only dreamt of during their working years.

From trekking through remote villages to sampling exotic cuisines, their travel adventures became stories that filled not just photo albums but their souls. Each destination etched a memory— moments of wonder, laughter, and shared experiences. Their dream to explore the world not only broadened their horizons but also strengthened their bond, marking retirement as the chapter of their most cherished adventures.

The Literary Legacy

After retiring from a corporate career, Daniel, at 68, pursued his lifelong dream of writing a novel. Though daunting, the desire to pen down stories that had lingered in his mind for years fueled his determination. He dedicated hours to crafting narratives, weaving characters and plots, diving into the world of storytelling.

Despite initial uncertainties, his perseverance paid off. His debut novel garnered praise and found its way onto bookshelves, delighting readers with tales that had brewed in his imagination. Daniel's dream of becoming a published author not only fulfilled a personal ambition but also inspired others to pursue their creative passions, proving that age was no barrier to artistic expression.

In the realm of dreams, age is but a number—an insignificant barrier in the face of unwavering determination and passion. Seniors who embark on this journey of pursuing dreams after retirement illustrate that dreams aren't bound by the constraints of youth but flourish through the wisdom, experience, and unwavering commitment that comes with age.

These stories are not just about personal triumphs but also about redefining the narrative of aging. They challenge stereotypes, inspiring others to break free from the shackles of limitations imposed by society and nurturing the belief that dreams are enduring companions, urging us forward regardless of the stage of life we're in.

The Musical Maestro

At 70, Henry's retirement marked the beginning of a musical journey he had postponed for decades. As a young man, he had a fervent love for playing the piano but had set it aside to focus on his career and family. With retirement came the opportunity to dust off his old piano and reignite his love for music.

Henry dedicated hours each day to practice, reconnecting with his favorite classical pieces and exploring new compositions. His passion for music grew, and he found himself performing at local gatherings and retirement communities. The joy he experienced while playing the piano was infectious, drawing audiences of all ages.

Beyond his personal fulfillment, Henry's story inspired others to revisit their abandoned passions. Through his music, he illustrated those dreams, no matter how long dormant, can be rekindled into roaring flames of passion and creativity.

The Culinary Explorer

After retiring from a successful career in engineering, John, at 68, decided to explore his passion for cooking. He enrolled in culinary classes, honing his skills and experimenting with flavors. At 70, he opened his own small café, showcasing his culinary creations. His determination and love for cooking transformed his retirement years into a flavorful adventure, proving that a passion for cuisine knows no age boundaries.

The Environmental Advocate

Following retirement from a teaching career, Sarah, at 67, dedicated herself to environmental advocacy. Her passion for conservation led her to volunteer at wildlife sanctuaries and advocate for eco-friendly practices in her community. Sarah's dedication inspired others, and at 72, she became a prominent voice in environmental activism, demonstrating that passion for a cause can drive meaningful change at any age.

The Community Builder

After retiring from a corporate job, Robert, at 63, pursued his dream of creating a community center for underprivileged youth. He invested his time and resources into building a safe space for children to learn and play. His efforts provided educational support and mentorship, positively impacting countless young lives. Robert's dream of fostering a supportive community for the next generation became a reality, showcasing the power of giving back in retirement.

In these stories of remarkable seniors pursuing their dreams after retirement, a resounding message emerges: dreams don't have an expiration date. These narratives stand as testaments to the enduring human spirit and the unwavering pursuit of passions, regardless of age or stage in life. They underscore the belief that the pursuit of dreams isn't confined to the earlier chapters of life but is a lifelong journey, waiting for the right moment to blossom into reality.

Through these inspiring tales, we witness the transformative power of resilience, determination, and unwavering commitment to one's aspirations. They serve as beacons of hope, igniting the spark within each of us to embrace our dreams, nurture our passions, and pave the way for an enriching, fulfilling life, reminding us that it's never too late to set sail towards the horizon of our aspirations, wherever they may lead.

Questions to Explore: Setting and Pursuing Dreams

1. **What drove these seniors to pursue their dreams after retirement?**

   - What motivated them to embark on these endeavors at a stage when many might perceive retirement as a time for relaxation?

2. **How did pursuing their dreams impact these seniors' overall well-being?**

   - In what ways did the pursuit of their dreams contribute to their mental, emotional, and physical health?

3. **What challenges did these seniors face while pursuing their dreams, and how did they overcome them?**

   - Did they encounter obstacles or doubts along the way? How did they navigate these challenges to continue pursuing their aspirations?

4. **What lessons can be learned from these seniors' stories of pursuing dreams after retirement?**

   - How can their experiences inspire and guide you, to follow your aspirations and dreams?

5. **How do these stories challenge the notion that dreams have an age limit?**

   - What do these narratives teach you about the enduring nature of dreams and the possibilities for personal fulfillment at any stage of life?

CHAPTER TWO SUMMARY

In the second chapter, "Setting and Pursuing Dreams," the narrative delves into the timeless concept of dreams and aspirations, highlighting their significance across all stages of life, including the senior years. The chapter serves as an inspiring exploration of the enduring nature of dreams, emphasizing that age should never be a barrier to pursuing one's passions and aspirations.

Through captivating stories, the chapter showcases real-life accounts of seniors who embarked on remarkable journeys after retirement. These narratives illustrate the resilience, determination, and unwavering spirit of seniors who refused to let age define or limit their aspirations. These individuals dared to pursue their dreams, whether it involved starting a new career, delving into a lifelong passion, or undertaking significant endeavors that fulfilled their deepest desires.

By presenting these compelling stories, "Setting and Pursuing Dreams" serves as a beacon of encouragement and motivation. It aims to inspire readers of all ages, encouraging them to recognize the enduring power of dreams and the endless possibilities that await, irrespective of their stage in life. The chapter embodies the idea that pursuing dreams is not confined by age but rather fueled by one's unwavering belief in the possibility of achieving them.

Ultimately, the chapter serves as an uplifting testament to the human spirit's resilience and the enduring nature of dreams. It instills a sense of hope, inspiring readers to nurture their aspirations and pursue their dreams passionately, regardless of any perceived limitations posed by age or circumstances.

CHAPTER 3

STAYING ACTIVE MIND-BODY-SPIRIT

Prioritizing Mental Stimulation and Lifelong Learning

For seniors, mental stimulation through lifelong learning is as vital as physical exercise. Engaging in activities like reading, learning new skills, or participating in educational courses fosters mental agility, stimulates curiosity, and supports cognitive health. Lifelong learning opens doors to new perspectives, sparks creativity, and nurtures a sense of continual growth and discovery.

Embracing Diverse Physical Activities for Seniors

Physical activity is crucial for seniors to maintain overall health. Gentle exercises like yoga, tai chi, or swimming offer benefits such as improved flexibility, balance, and cardiovascular health. Incorporating strength training using resistance bands or light weights helps maintain muscle mass and bone density. Daily walks, dancing, or group fitness classes not only keep the body active but also promote social engagement, which is essential for emotional well-being.

Mind, Body, and Soul

Meet Sarah, a retired teacher in her late 70s. After retiring, she refused to let her mind grow idle. She enrolled in local community college courses, exploring topics she had always been curious about but never had the time to delve into. Through history classes and creative writing workshops, Sarah found herself invigorated, her mind buzzing with newfound knowledge and ideas. She felt a renewed sense of purpose, cherishing the mental stimulation that these courses brought into her life.

But Sarah's journey didn't end with mental stimulation alone. Understanding the importance of physical activity, she embraced yoga and tai chi classes at the local senior center. These activities not only enhanced her flexibility and balance but also provided a sense of tranquility and mindfulness. As she progressed, she felt a deeper connection between her mind and body, experiencing a harmonious balance that brought immense joy and vitality to her senior years.

Finding and Nurturing Faith as a Senior

Finding faith as a senior can involve introspection and exploration. It might include attending religious services, joining study groups, or seeking guidance from spiritual mentors. Exploring various faith practices, readings, and contemplation aids in strengthening one's spiritual beliefs and understanding.

Using Faith in Daily Life

Using faith involves integrating its principles into daily life. Many seniors find solace and guidance through prayer, meditation, or contemplation. Applying the values of compassion, forgiveness, and gratitude in interactions reflects the essence of faith traditions, fostering a sense of purpose and peace.

Active Faith Through Community and Service

Active faith often involves community engagement and service. Connecting with others who share similar beliefs through religious congregations or participating in communal activities provides support and a sense of belonging.

Engaging in acts of service, volunteering, or supporting charitable causes aligns with many faith teachings, offering fulfillment and a sense of contributing positively to society.

By prioritizing mental stimulation, diverse physical activities, and embracing faith, seniors can lead fulfilling and vibrant lives, nurturing their minds, bodies, and spirits throughout their golden years.

Seeking and Exploring Faith

As a senior, discovering or deepening faith involves exploration. This might include attending religious services, participating in study groups, or seeking counsel from spiritual mentors or leaders. Exploring different practices, readings, and discussions helps in understanding and nurturing one's spiritual beliefs and traditions.

Incorporating Faith in Daily Life

Once faith is discovered or affirmed, it's about integrating its teachings into daily routines. Many seniors find solace and strength through prayer, meditation, or contemplation. Embracing the values of kindness, compassion, and forgiveness in daily interactions reflects the essence of many faith traditions and contributes to a sense of purpose and harmony.

Finding Community and Connection

For seniors, faith often offers a sense of community and belonging. Connecting with others who share similar beliefs through religious gatherings, community services, or outreach programs provides support and a sense of shared purpose, fostering meaningful connections and a sense of unity.

Service and Contribution

Using faith often involves service and contribution. Volunteering, supporting charitable causes, or engaging in acts of kindness align with many faith teachings. Seniors often find fulfillment and purpose by contributing positively to their communities, fostering a sense of fulfillment and leaving a positive impact.

Embracing Spiritual Growth

Activating faith involves continuous spiritual growth. It includes seeking deeper understanding, reflecting on beliefs, and embracing the evolving nature of spirituality in daily life. This journey of faith often leads to personal growth, providing guidance, strength, and a sense of direction.

John, a retired businessman in his 80s, found solace and strength in his faith community after his wife passed away. He had always been a devout churchgoer but had never actively engaged beyond attending services. However, after his loss, John felt the need for deeper spiritual connection and community. He started volunteering at his church's outreach programs, delivering meals to the elderly and participating in discussions about faith and life's purpose.

As John became more involved, he realized that his faith wasn't just a part of his life; it was his life. The sense of belonging and purpose he found in helping others brought immense satisfaction. His faith became an anchor, guiding him through grief and providing a foundation of hope and resilience. John's newfound active engagement in his faith community not only nourished his spirit but also had a profound positive impact on his mental and emotional well-being.

These stories highlight how staying active in mind, body, and spirit isn't just about physical exercise or mental stimulation alone. It's about embracing a holistic approach to senior wellness, encompassing intellectual curiosity, physical activities, and spiritual engagement, leading to a fulfilling and vibrant life in the golden years.

Embrace the Journey

In embracing the journey of staying active in mind, body, and spirit as seniors, it's crucial to recognize the interconnectedness of these elements. The pursuit of lifelong learning and mental stimulation isn't simply cerebral exercise; it invigorates the soul and keeps the spirit vibrant. Engaging in diverse physical activities tailored to individual abilities isn't solely about keeping the body fit; it nurtures emotional well-being and cultivates a sense of community through shared experiences.

Furthermore, the pursuit of faith isn't an isolated practice but an integral part of this holistic approach. Finding, using, and activating faith as a senior isn't just about religious observances; it's about discovering a deeper connection, a source of strength that permeates through every aspect of life. It's in this holistic tapestry of mental, physical, and spiritual engagement that seniors uncover a roadmap to a fulfilling and vibrant life, each element complementing and enriching the other, creating a symphony of well-being that echoes through the golden years.

Questions to Explore: Staying Active: Mind Body and Spirit

1. **Mind**

   - How can I challenge my mind today? What new skill or knowledge can I explore to keep my mind active and engaged?

   - What intellectual pursuit or hobby can I incorporate into my routine to stimulate my cognitive abilities and foster continuous learning?

2. **Body**

   - What physical activities bring me joy and promote my well-being? How can I integrate these activities into my daily or weekly routine?

   - In what ways can I adapt exercises to suit my abilities and ensure my body remains active and healthy?

3. **Spirit**

   - How does spirituality or faith play a role in my daily life? How can I nurture this aspect to enhance my sense of purpose and connection?

   - Are there rituals, practices, or community engagements within my faith or spirituality that bring me peace and fulfillment?

4. **Integration**

   - How can I find a balance between mental, physical, and spiritual activities to create a holistic approach to wellness?

   - Are there connections between my mental pursuits, physical activities, and spiritual practices that I can explore to enhance their collective impact on my well-being?

5. **Growth and Adaptation**

   - How can I adapt my routines to accommodate changes in my abilities or interests, ensuring a continued focus on mental, physical, and spiritual wellness?

   - What steps can I take today to foster growth in each aspect—mind, body, and spirit—to ensure a fulfilling and vibrant life in my senior year

CHAPTER THREE SUMMARY

In the comprehensive chapter titled "Staying Active: Mind and Body," the narrative centers on the holistic well-being of seniors, emphasizing the integral connection between mental stimulation, lifelong learning, and physical activities tailored to their needs.

The chapter meticulously delves into the significance of mental stimulation as a crucial component of healthy aging. It advocates for continuous learning and engagement, encouraging seniors to explore various avenues for mental exercise such as reading, puzzles, arts, and lifelong learning programs. This emphasis on mental agility serves as a foundation for maintaining cognitive sharpness and fostering a sense of intellectual fulfillment.

Furthermore, the chapter meticulously discusses a diverse array of physical activities specifically curated for seniors. It elaborates on the importance of staying physically active, outlining exercises and activities designed to cater to their abilities and preferences. From low-impact exercises like yoga, tai chi, and gentle aerobics to outdoor activities such as walking, swimming, and gardening, the chapter provides a comprehensive guide tailored to promoting physical well-being.

Moreover, the narrative underscores the interplay between mental and physical health, advocating that a balanced regimen encompassing both aspects is pivotal for optimal senior health. By fostering mental stimulation and engaging in suitable physical activities, seniors can enhance their overall well-being and maintain a fulfilling lifestyle.

"Staying Active: Mind and Body" emerges as a comprehensive resource, offering actionable insights and guidance to seniors seeking to lead an active and fulfilling life. It champions the idea that remaining mentally and physically engaged is not just beneficial but integral to a vibrant and healthy senior lifestyle. Through its meticulous exploration of activities and exercises, the chapter serves as a roadmap for seniors, inspiring them to embark on a journey of lifelong learning and physical well-being.

OVERCOMING CHALLENGES AND EMBRACING CHANGE

Navigating the senior years often presents a unique set of challenges that require adaptation and resilience. One prevalent hurdle is the shift in roles and routines upon retirement, where the structured work-life gives way to newfound freedom. This transition can sometimes lead to feelings of purposelessness or isolation. Overcoming this challenge involves exploring new interests, volunteering, or pursuing lifelong passions. Embracing retirement as an opportunity for personal growth and exploration can rekindle a sense of purpose and fulfillment.

Health concerns are another significant challenge. Aging often brings various health issues, both physical and mental. However, proactive measures like maintaining a healthy lifestyle, regular exercise, balanced nutrition, and seeking medical guidance can mitigate many health challenges. Embracing change means adapting one's routines to accommodate these changes while not letting them define or limit life experiences.

Social isolation can also be daunting for seniors, especially after significant life changes. Building and nurturing social connections become imperative. Engaging in community activities, joining clubs, attending social gatherings, or utilizing technology for virtual connections can help combat isolation and foster a sense of belonging.

Furthermore, the loss of loved ones and friends is a natural part of aging but can be emotionally taxing. Coping with grief involves acknowledging and processing these emotions. Seeking support through counseling, support groups, or leaning on close relationships aids in navigating this challenging terrain.

Lastly, financial concerns often weigh heavily on seniors. Budgeting wisely, seeking financial advice, and exploring opportunities for part-time work or volunteer positions can alleviate these worries. Embracing change in financial situations involves proactive planning and adapting to evolving circumstances.

Embracing change and overcoming challenges in the senior years necessitates a resilient mindset. It's about acknowledging these hurdles, seeking support, and adopting strategies to adapt and thrive. Maintaining flexibility, cultivating a positive outlook, and embracing new experiences pave the way for a fulfilling and enriching life in the later years.

Rediscovering Purpose

Meet James, who, after retiring from his lifelong career, found himself adrift without the structure of work. Initially feeling purposeless, he discovered a passion for woodworking. He spent hours crafting intricate pieces, volunteering to teach woodworking at a local community center. Through this newfound interest, James found renewed purpose and fulfillment, transforming his retirement into an exciting chapter of creativity and community contribution.

Conquering Health Challenge

Mary faced health challenges as she aged, including arthritis that limited her mobility. Determined not to let it define her, she embraced gentle yoga and aquatic therapy, adapting these exercises to suit her abilities. With dedication and perseverance, Mary not only managed her health condition but also found a vibrant community among fellow yoga enthusiasts, fostering a sense of camaraderie and physical well-being.

Bridging Social Isolation

John, recently widowed, grappled with loneliness. Instead of withdrawing, he joined a local seniors' club, attending weekly meetings and outings. Through these activities, he formed deep friendships, sharing experiences and supporting one another through life's changes. John discovered that by opening himself to new connections, he could combat isolation and build a supportive network.

Navigating Loss and Grief

After losing her lifelong partner, Sarah found solace in a grief support group. Sharing her emotions and experiences with others navigating similar loss helped her process her grief. Sarah discovered that acknowledging and sharing her feelings in a supportive environment brought comfort and healing, allowing her to navigate her journey of loss with resilience.

Overcoming Financial Worries

Facing financial uncertainties post-retirement, Michael sought advice from a financial advisor. With prudent budgeting and exploring part-time consulting opportunities, he managed to alleviate his worries. Michael learned that proactive planning and seeking guidance enabled him to adapt to changing financial circumstances, bringing stability and peace of mind.

These stories exemplify how seniors confront and overcome challenges in their later years by embracing change, seeking support, and adopting strategies that empower them to lead fulfilling and resilient lives.

Adapting to Change

Adapting to change and fostering resilience is pivotal, especially in the later years, where life transitions become more frequent and substantial. One of the key facets of resilience is understanding that change is inevitable and embracing it as an opportunity for growth. It's not merely about weathering the storm but learning to dance in the rain. Resilient individuals often display an adaptive mindset, readily accepting change and actively seeking ways to navigate it positively.

Moreover, staying resilient involves acknowledging the emotional impact of change while maintaining a forward-looking perspective. Life events like retirement, loss of loved ones, or health challenges can be disruptive, but resilient individuals use these moments to reassess priorities and cultivate new goals. They exhibit flexibility, adjusting their sails to navigate the winds of change, rather than being rigidly anchored in past routines.

Resilience isn't about avoiding hardship but bouncing back stronger after facing adversity. It involves building a toolkit of coping mechanisms and support networks. Seniors who maintain resilience often engage in activities that foster mental agility, such as reading, learning new skills, or pursuing hobbies. These activities bolster cognitive flexibility and emotional strength, enabling them to adapt more effectively to change.

Moreover, resilient individuals understand the importance of seeking and offering support. They lean on trusted friends, family, or community resources when facing challenges. Conversely, they also extend a helping hand, contributing to others' well-being. This reciprocity creates a network of support that acts as a cushion during turbulent times.

Lastly, resilience is grounded in self-care. Seniors who prioritize self-care—be it through physical exercise, healthy habits, mindfulness practices, or pursuing passions—cultivate inner strength. By nurturing their well-being, they enhance their capacity to face and overcome life's uncertainties.

In essence, adapting to change and staying resilient in the senior years is about fostering an attitude of flexibility, proactivity, and self-care. It's about accepting change as a natural part of life, learning from it, and emerging stronger, more adaptable, and wiser from the experiences encountered along the way.

In the tapestry of life, the ability to adapt to change and display resilience forms the cornerstone of personal growth and fortitude. These stories exemplify the human spirit's capacity to weather storms, pivot in the face of adversity, and emerge stronger from life's unexpected twists and turns. They underscore that while change may be inevitable, our response to it determines our trajectory.

Ultimately, these tales serve as testaments to the enduring power of the human spirit. They remind us that amidst the winds of change, resilience isn't just about bouncing back; it's about growing, evolving, and flourishing in the face of life's unpredictability. As these individuals embraced change, navigated adversity, and displayed unwavering resilience, they paved the way for inspiration and hope, showcasing the indomitable strength of the human resolve.

Questions to Explore:

Overcoming Challenges and Embracing Change

1. What strategies have you found most effective in overcoming common challenges faced by seniors, such as adapting to retirement or managing health changes? How do you navigate these transitions?

2. How important do you think resilience is in navigating life changes as a senior? Can you share an experience where resilience played a crucial role in adapting to a significant life change?

3. In what ways do you actively seek to adapt to change and embrace new experiences in your senior years? How do you foster a positive attitude toward change and uncertainty?

4. How do you handle the emotional aspects of change, such as dealing with loss, adjusting to a new lifestyle, or facing health challenges? Are there specific coping mechanisms or support systems you find helpful?

5. Reflecting on your experiences, can you share a story where overcoming a challenge or adapting to change in your senior years brought unexpected growth or new opportunities into your life? How did this experience impact your perspective on change and resilience.

CHAPTER FOUR SUMMARY

In the illuminating chapter titled "Overcoming Challenges and Embracing Change," the narrative delves deeply into the unique hurdles encountered by seniors, offering insightful strategies to navigate these obstacles while embracing resilience in the face of change.

The chapter empathetically addresses the prevalent challenges that often accompany the senior years, acknowledging the multifaceted nature of these difficulties. From transitions into retirement to health concerns, social isolation, loss, and financial worries, the narrative compassionately explores each challenge faced by seniors.

Moreover, the chapter serves as a beacon of guidance, offering practical advice and approaches to overcome these challenges. It doesn't merely acknowledge the obstacles but actively provides strategies for adaptation and resilience. It underscores the importance of adapting to change, advocating for a flexible mindset that enables seniors to navigate life's transitions more effectively.

Furthermore, the narrative accentuates the significance of resilience as a crucial attribute in confronting challenges. It explores how seniors can cultivate resilience, emphasizing the power of a positive outlook, social support systems, and proactive coping mechanisms to confront and overcome obstacles.

"Overcoming Challenges and Embracing Change" emerges as a supportive guide, acknowledging the complexities of aging while offering invaluable insights to seniors. It promotes the idea that while challenges are inevitable, they need not define or limit one's experiences. Instead, the chapter empowers seniors to face adversity with resilience, adaptability, and an unwavering spirit, fostering a sense of empowerment and assurance amid life's transitions.

TRANSFORMATION THROUGH FAITH AND MINDSET

Transformation through faith and mindset plays a profound role in the lives of seniors, fostering a sense of purpose, hope, and resilience. For many, faith serves as an anchor, providing strength and guidance through life's trials. Whether rooted in religious beliefs or spirituality, faith often acts as a source of solace, offering comfort and a sense of connection to something larger than oneself.

Moreover, a positive mindset is a powerful catalyst for personal growth, irrespective of age. Seniors who cultivate a positive outlook often find themselves embracing new opportunities, overcoming obstacles, and approaching life with enthusiasm. This mindset shift allows them to see challenges as stepping stones for growth rather than insurmountable barriers, leading to transformation in various aspects of their lives.

The intertwining of faith and a positive mindset offers seniors a pathway toward inner transformation. It enables them to tap into their inner strength, fostering resilience in times of adversity. This transformation isn't solely about monumental changes but also about the subtle shifts in perspective, enabling seniors to find joy in simple moments, nurture relationships, and explore new passions, ultimately leading to a more fulfilling life.

Regardless of age, seniors undergoing transformation through faith and mindset often exhibit a greater sense of gratitude, compassion, and empathy. They discover a renewed sense of purpose, embracing life's journey with a spirit of openness and acceptance. This transformation isn't about erasing the challenges of aging but about embracing them with grace, using these experiences as opportunities for personal evolution and enlightenment.

In essence, the intertwining of faith and a positive mindset serves as a beacon of light in the lives of seniors, guiding them toward transformation, growth, and a deeper appreciation for the richness of life, allowing them to navigate the later years with resilience, optimism, and a sense of fulfillment.

The Power of Faith

Sarah, a senior who, after facing a series of health setbacks, found solace and strength in her unwavering faith. Despite the challenges, Sarah's belief became her cornerstone, guiding her through difficult times. Through prayer, meditation, and active involvement in her faith community, she discovered resilience and peace. Her faith not only supported her emotionally but also inspired those around her. Sarah's steadfast belief transformed her perspective on life's challenges, fostering a sense of hope and resilience that carried her through adversity.

Embracing a Positive Mindset

Julius, in his senior years, found himself with newfound time after retirement. Rather than viewing this as an endpoint, he embraced it as a fresh beginning. Through positive affirmations, daily gratitude practices, and actively seeking new hobbies, John nurtured a positive mindset. He immersed himself in lifelong learning, engaging in painting classes and learning a musical instrument. This shift in perspective revitalized his life, instilling a sense of joy and enthusiasm that allowed him to grow, learn, and thrive in his later years.

Transformation through Community and Faith Maria, a retiree, experienced a profound transformation through her involvement in her faith community. Volunteering at a local shelter and actively participating in communal prayer sessions became the cornerstone of her spiritual growth. Her engagement in these activities not only brought her a sense of fulfillment but also strengthened her connection with others. This sense of belonging and purpose transformed Maria's outlook, inspiring her to spread positivity and kindness in her community, contributing to her personal growth and a deeper sense of fulfillment.

Faith as a Source of Strength

Susan, a retiree, faced a series of health challenges that left her feeling despondent. Turning to her faith, she found solace in daily meditation and prayer. Through her spiritual practices, Sarah discovered an inner resilience that helped her navigate difficult times. Her unwavering faith not only provided comfort but also instilled in her the strength to embrace each day with gratitude and hope. This newfound mindset enabled Sarah to view her health challenges as opportunities for personal growth and spiritual deepening, ultimately leading to a remarkable transformation in her outlook on life.

Embracing Positivity Amidst Change

Joel, in his late seventies, found himself grappling with loneliness after the passing of his spouse. Determined not to succumb to despair, he turned to the power of positive thinking. Through daily affirmations and gratitude practices, John cultivated a more optimistic mindset. He started volunteering at a local community center, fostering new connections and a renewed sense of purpose. His positive outlook not only helped him navigate the grieving process but also led to personal growth, allowing him to find joy and fulfillment in building new relationships and contributing to his community.

Finding Resilience Through Faith

Rebecca, an octogenarian, faced financial hardships after unforeseen circumstances. Despite the challenges, she held steadfast to her faith. Through prayer and meditation, Rebecca found the inner strength to navigate the uncertainties. Her unwavering faith instilled in her a sense of resilience, enabling her to adapt to her changed circumstances. Rather than succumbing to despair, Rebecca approached her situation with a positive mindset, seeking opportunities to rebuild and recalibrate her life. Her faith became a guiding force in transforming her perspective on adversity, leading to personal growth and a newfound sense of resilience in her twilight years.

These stories illuminate how faith and a positive mindset serve as catalysts for personal growth and transformation in seniors' lives, showcasing their ability to find strength, resilience, and renewal regardless of life's challenges.

The intertwining journey of faith and a positive mindset in seniors' lives is an enduring testament to the resilience of the human spirit. Through these narratives of personal growth and transformation, it becomes evident that age does not limit the capacity for inner change and renewal. Rather, it showcases the immense power of faith and a positive mindset to guide individuals toward resilience, hope, and newfound purpose.

As seniors navigate the complexities of life, their stories illuminate a profound truth: that faith, coupled with a positive outlook, isn't just an antidote to life's adversities but a beacon guiding them toward continual growth and transformation. These narratives remind us that regardless of age, the pursuit of a deeper understanding of oneself and the world is an ongoing journey—one marked by the unwavering belief in the possibilities of personal evolution and the embrace of a mindset that fuels resilience, strength, and inner peace.

Questions to Explore:

Transformation Through Faith and Mindset

1. How has faith or spirituality influenced your perspective on aging and personal growth? Have there been moments where your beliefs guided you through challenging times, fostering resilience and personal transformation?

2. In what ways do you nurture a positive mindset in your daily life? How does maintaining a positive outlook contribute to your overall well-being and sense of purpose, regardless of life's circumstances?

3. Reflecting on your journey, can you recall a time when faith or a positive mindset played a pivotal role in helping you overcome a significant obstacle or adapt to a major life change? How did this experience impact your outlook on life?

4. How do you intertwine faith, spirituality, or a positive mindset with your pursuit of personal growth and continual learning as you navigate your senior years? Are there specific practices or beliefs that guide you on this journey?

5. In what ways has the evolution of your beliefs or mindset influenced your approach to aging? How does embracing faith or cultivating a positive mindset contribute to your

sense of fulfillment, purpose, and resilience as you grow older?

CHAPTER FIVE SUMMARY

In the thought-provoking chapter titled "Transformation Through Faith and Mindset," the narrative takes a profound dive into the intrinsic relationship between faith, mindset, and personal growth in the lives of seniors, presenting a powerful exploration of these influential aspects.

The chapter meticulously explores the profound impact of faith and a positive mindset on the lives of seniors, irrespective of religious affiliation. It delves into the transformative power of faith, illustrating how beliefs and spiritual practices provide strength, hope, and resilience to navigate life's challenges. Furthermore, it highlights how a positive mindset, coupled with faith-based perspectives, contributes to mental fortitude, fostering a sense of purpose, and enabling seniors to approach life's transitions with renewed optimism.

Moreover, the chapter reflects on personal growth and transformation, emphasizing that these processes are not confined by age. It encourages seniors to embark on a journey of continuous self-improvement, advocating for a mindset that embraces change and seeks new opportunities for growth and development.

Additionally, the narrative provides insights into how faith and a positive mindset can catalyze personal transformation, inspiring seniors to redefine their outlook on life and embrace a renewed sense of purpose. It underscores the potential for profound inner growth, regardless of the chronological age, by nurturing faith-based beliefs and fostering a positive mental attitude.

"Transformation Through Faith and Mindset" emerges as an empowering chapter, celebrating the enduring influence of faith and a positive mindset on seniors' lives. It invites readers to reflect on their belief systems, encouraging them to cultivate a positive perspective and embrace personal growth, thereby fostering resilience and finding renewed meaning and fulfillment in their later years.

CHAPTER 6

THE POWER OF LOVE AND ACCEPTANCE

In the tapestry of senior life, the significance of love, acceptance, and inclusivity weaves a vibrant pattern that nurtures a supportive and thriving community. The power of love among seniors transcends mere affection; it extends to empathy, compassion, and a profound understanding of one another's journeys. Within this realm, fostering an environment of acceptance becomes paramount—a space where differences are celebrated, and individuals are valued for their unique experiences and perspectives.

Love and acceptance among seniors serve as pillars that uphold a community's spirit, enabling individuals to forge connections beyond mere acquaintanceship. These connections are rooted in mutual respect, kindness, and a genuine interest in one another's well-being. In such an environment, seniors feel seen, heard, and embraced for who they are, fostering a sense of belonging and camaraderie that enriches their lives.

Embracing inclusivity within senior communities further enhances the tapestry of love and acceptance. It's about acknowledging and celebrating the diversity of backgrounds, cultures, and beliefs among seniors. Inclusivity fosters an environment where everyone feels welcome, valued, and understood, transcending barriers and creating bridges of understanding and empathy.

Encouraging a positive, supportive community among seniors is not merely about fostering amicable relationships but about creating a nurturing space where individuals can thrive. It's about cultivating an atmosphere that promotes mental, emotional, and social well-being, allowing seniors to navigate the intricacies of aging with grace, support, and a sense of collective purpose.

Ultimately, the power of love, acceptance, and inclusivity among seniors isn't just about creating harmonious connections; it's about nurturing a community where individuals feel cherished, respected, and empowered—a community where every voice is heard, every story is valued, and every heart is embraced.

The Knitting Circle of Inclusivity

In a quaint retirement community, a group of seniors gathers every week for what they affectionately call the "Knitting Circle." This circle isn't just about yarn and needles; it's a sanctuary of warmth, acceptance, and inclusivity. Margaret, one of the circle's founders, recalls how the group started small but gradually expanded to include seniors from diverse backgrounds. Their gatherings transcend knitting—they share stories, experiences, and laughter. The circle has become a haven where differences are embraced, and each member is valued for their unique contributions. From discussing life lessons to lending a helping hand during tough times, this inclusive community embodies the essence of love, acceptance, and supportive camaraderie among seniors.

The Garden of Acceptance

At a senior living facility, a once-barren garden became a symbol of unity and acceptance. Residents of varied ethnicities, backgrounds, and abilities came together to transform the neglected space into a vibrant oasis. Maria, a retired teacher, brought her gardening expertise and encouraged others to join. As the garden bloomed, so did friendships. Each senior contributed in their own way—planting, watering, and nurturing. Through this shared endeavor, barriers dissolved, and a sense of belonging flourished. The garden became a place where acceptance blossomed, where every plant, like every person, was cherished for its unique beauty. It stood as a testament to the power of collective effort and inclusivity in forging a supportive community among seniors.

The Book Club of Understanding

In a retirement home, a book club became a sanctuary for understanding and empathy. Led by Charles, a retired librarian, the club attracted seniors from diverse walks of life. As they delved into different literary worlds, they discovered connections that transcended age and backgrounds. Discussions went beyond the book—they shared personal stories, reflecting on life experiences. It became a safe space for open dialogue and mutual respect. Through listening and understanding each other's perspectives, the club exemplified how love, acceptance, and inclusivity foster a positive, supportive community among seniors. They showed that sharing stories, experiences, and emotions binds individuals together, creating a tapestry of empathy and support.

These stories vividly portray the transformative power of love, acceptance, and inclusivity in nurturing a positive, supportive community among seniors, where differences are celebrated, bonds are formed, and each individual is embraced for their uniqueness.

The Harmony of Cultural Exchange

In a senior living complex, a weekly cultural exchange gathering became the cornerstone of connection and understanding among residents. Every Friday, seniors from various ethnic backgrounds gathered to celebrate diversity through food, music, and traditions. Maria, an Italian immigrant, often brought homemade pasta dishes, while Mr. Patel, originally from India, showcased his mastery in preparing traditional spices. These gatherings were not just about sharing cuisines; they were a celebration of each other's heritage. Over time, the exchange evolved into a space of deep camaraderie and mutual respect. It served as a testament to the power of embracing differences and fostering inclusivity among seniors, creating a nurturing environment where cultural diversity was cherished and celebrated.

The Artistic Unity Project

A retired art teacher, Mrs. Lewis, initiated an art project in the senior community center, inviting seniors to collaborate on a mural. Despite varying artistic skills, each senior contributed their unique touch to the artwork. The mural depicted scenes from their lives, intertwining diverse perspectives and experiences. What began as a simple painting endeavor transformed into a powerful symbol of unity and acceptance. Through this project, seniors discovered the joy of collaborative creation and learned to appreciate the beauty in differences. The mural not only adorned the center's walls but also became a constant reminder of the strength found in embracing diversity and fostering a positive, supportive community among seniors.

The Wisdom Circle

In a retirement village, a group of seniors formed what they fondly called the "Wisdom Circle." Here, seniors gathered to share their life experiences, insights, and advice with one another. The circle became a melting pot of wisdom, where each individual's journey was respected and valued. From tales of triumph over adversity to sharing lessons learned through hardships, these gatherings fostered empathy, understanding, and acceptance. The circle wasn't just about imparting wisdom; it was a space where seniors felt heard, understood, and embraced for their unique life paths. Through this mutual exchange, the Wisdom Circle exemplified how love, acceptance, and inclusivity create a nurturing and supportive community where the richness of life experiences is treasured.

These stories illuminate the significance of love, acceptance, and inclusivity among seniors, showcasing how these values contribute to building a positive, supportive environment where diversity is celebrated, connections flourish, and mutual respect thrives.

Embracing a Tapestry of Love and Inclusivity

In the colorful mosaic of senior life, love, acceptance, and inclusivity weave threads that create a vibrant tapestry of communal support. The power of these values is not merely seen but felt deeply within the interconnected lives of seniors. Love transcends boundaries, dissolving differences and fostering connections that resonate beyond words. It's the warmth of a welcoming smile, the comfort of a compassionate ear, and the shared laughter that binds hearts together. Acceptance becomes the cornerstone of understanding, where individuals, irrespective of backgrounds, are embraced for their uniqueness. In this realm of inclusivity, diversity flourishes, each thread contributing to the richness of the fabric. Every senior, like a distinct thread, weaves into the fabric of community, creating a tapestry that symbolizes unity amid diversity.

The significance of cultivating a community rooted in love, acceptance, and inclusivity cannot be overstated. It's in these values that seniors find solace during challenging times, strength in the support of their peers, and joy in shared experiences. A positive, supportive community doesn't merely happen; it's nurtured by the collective efforts of individuals who value empathy, kindness, and understanding. It's a space where differences are acknowledged, celebrated, and woven together to create a resilient and beautiful fabric of communal life.

A Symphony of Support and Connection

The essence of a positive, supportive community among seniors is akin to a symphony—a harmonious blend of diverse melodies coming together to create a masterpiece. Love orchestrates this symphony, infusing each note with empathy, compassion, and camaraderie. Acceptance forms the melody, a song that resonates with understanding, allowing each senior's unique tune to be heard and appreciated. Inclusivity becomes the rhythm, binding these tunes together, creating a symphony of belonging and unity. Within this musical ensemble of community life, seniors find a place where their stories, experiences, and aspirations harmonize to create a beautiful composition of shared existence.

Encouraging a positive, supportive community is about conducting this symphony of connection. It's about fostering an environment where seniors feel valued, respected, and understood. It's providing the space for conversations that transcend differences, where laughter mingles with shared wisdom, creating a melody that uplifts spirits. A supportive community is a sanctuary where hearts resonate with compassion and souls find resonance in collective support. It's a testament to the strength found in unity, in coming together to compose a masterpiece of communal life.

These concluding chapters encapsulate the pivotal role of love, acceptance, inclusivity, and a supportive environment in creating a thriving and vibrant community among seniors, where the beauty of diversity is celebrated, connections flourish, and hearts find solace in shared experiences.

Questions to Explore: The Power of Love and Acceptance

1. How does fostering an environment of love and acceptance among seniors contribute to your emotional well-being and overall quality of life?

2. In what ways can inclusivity and embracing diversity among seniors strengthen their sense of belonging and create a more supportive community environment?

3. What role does empathy play in cultivating a positive and inclusive atmosphere among seniors, fostering connections and understanding?

4. How can a community that values acceptance and inclusivity among seniors empower you to share your unique experiences, creating a tapestry of wisdom and mutual support?

5. How does a culture of love, acceptance, and inclusivity among seniors positively impact intergenerational relationships and interactions within the broader community?

CHAPTER SIX SUMMARY

In the captivating chapter titled "The Power of Love and Acceptance," the narrative delves deeply into the profound significance of fostering love, acceptance, and inclusivity within the senior community, advocating for the creation of a nurturing and supportive environment.

The chapter intricately explores the vital role played by love and acceptance in enhancing the well-being of seniors. It underscores the transformative impact of fostering an environment rich in love and compassion, highlighting how these elements contribute to emotional resilience, mental well-being, and a sense of belonging among seniors.

Furthermore, the chapter passionately advocates for inclusivity within the senior community, emphasizing the importance of embracing diversity and celebrating individual differences. It showcases how an inclusive environment fosters a sense of community where each senior feels valued, respected, and embraced for their uniqueness.

Moreover, the narrative encourages the cultivation of a positive, supportive community among seniors. It explores ways to build meaningful connections, emphasizing the power of camaraderie and mutual support. It celebrates initiatives that promote collaboration, empathy, and understanding among seniors, fostering a sense of solidarity and togetherness.

"The Power of Love and Acceptance" emerges as an inspiring chapter, advocating for an environment where love, acceptance, and inclusivity reign supreme. It serves as a heartfelt call to action, urging seniors to foster a community that embodies empathy, kindness, and mutual respect. Ultimately, the chapter emphasizes that through the cultivation of a positive and supportive environment, seniors can experience enhanced well-being, fulfillment, and a deeper sense of connection with their community.

TAKING ACTION AND CHANGING THE WORLD

Embracing the Power of Purposeful Action

Seniors hold a wealth of experiences, wisdom, and knowledge, and their actions possess the potential to create significant ripples of change. Each day presents an opportunity to embark on a journey of transformation, not just for personal growth but also for the betterment of communities. Embracing change begins with recognizing the strength within oneself to effect positive shifts. Seniors can channel their life experiences and expertise into meaningful actions, leading the way toward a brighter future for themselves and the world around them.

Initiating Change, Inspiring Others

The decision to instigate change, no matter how small, ignites a chain reaction that inspires others. Seniors can serve as catalysts for transformation by undertaking initiatives that promote well-being, inclusivity, and progress. Whether it's starting community programs, mentoring younger generations, or advocating for social causes, each action becomes a stepping stone toward a more compassionate and equitable society. Seniors, through their commitment and determination, become beacons of inspiration, encouraging others to join in the pursuit of positive change.

Community Engagement and Impactful Change

Engaging actively within their communities empowers seniors to bring about impactful change. By volunteering, leading discussions, or organizing local events, seniors create platforms for dialogue and unity. Such engagements foster a sense of belonging, enriching the lives of both the individuals involved and the broader community. Initiatives that promote solidarity, resilience, and compassion have the power to transform neighborhoods and instill a sense of pride and purpose among seniors.

Embracing Transformation for Personal Fulfillment

Change isn't solely about the external impact; it's also about personal growth and fulfillment. Seniors who embrace change often discover renewed purpose and a deeper sense of fulfillment. By pursuing new passions, learning novel skills, or engaging in creative endeavors, they embark on a journey of self-discovery and enrichment. This personal transformation not only enhances their own lives but also radiates positivity, inspiring others to embark on their own transformative journeys.

Leaving a Lasting Legacy of Change

Seniors have the remarkable opportunity to leave behind a legacy of positive change. Every action taken, every seed of change sown, contributes to a legacy that transcends time. Through their actions, seniors imprint their values and aspirations onto future generations, leaving an indelible mark on society. By embracing change and taking proactive steps toward a better world, seniors shape a legacy rooted in compassion, resilience, and a profound commitment to making the world a better place for generations to come.

The Community Revival Project

In a close-knit neighborhood, a group of seniors embarked on a project to revitalize their community park. Led by James, a retired architect, the group envisioned a space that would bring people together. They organized fundraising events, engaged local volunteers, and worked tirelessly to refurbish the neglected park. What started as a modest effort soon blossomed into a thriving community hub. The park became a place where families gathered, children played, and neighbors forged bonds. The seniors' dedication and passion not only transformed a neglected area but also revitalized the spirit of the entire neighborhood, inspiring others to take pride in their community and initiate positive changes.

The Wellness Initiative

Mary, a retired nurse, noticed a lack of health awareness programs for seniors in her area. Determined to address this, she initiated a wellness initiative aimed at promoting healthy living among seniors. She organized workshops on nutrition, exercise routines suitable for different abilities, and mental well-being sessions. Seniors embraced these sessions, forming support groups and encouraging one another to lead healthier lifestyles. As a result, the initiative not only improved the physical and mental health of participants but also fostered a strong sense of camaraderie. Mary's dedication and commitment inspired other seniors to take charge of their health and empowered them to make positive changes in their lives.

The Intergenerational Mentorship Program

A group of retired professionals, led by Richard, recognized the untapped potential in fostering connections between seniors and younger generations. They established an intergenerational mentorship program where seniors volunteered to mentor local youth. The program paired seniors' wisdom and experience with the enthusiasm and innovation of the younger generation. Through this mentorship, seniors shared valuable life lessons, career guidance, and personal experiences, while the younger mentees offered insights into modern technologies and changing societal trends. The exchange of knowledge and perspectives not only benefited the mentees but also rejuvenated the seniors, giving them a renewed sense of purpose. This initiative encouraged other seniors to embrace change, engage with younger generations, and contribute meaningfully to their communities.

The Sustainable Living Initiative

In a retirement community, a group of environmentally-conscious seniors led by Thomas, a retired environmentalist, initiated a sustainable living project. They implemented various eco-friendly practices within their community, such as composting, rainwater harvesting, and promoting energy-efficient measures. Their efforts not only reduced the community's environmental footprint but also inspired neighboring areas to adopt similar practices. Through workshops and community events, they shared their knowledge and experiences, motivating others to embrace sustainable living practices, thus making a collective impact on the environment.

The Empowerment through Education Program

Evelyn, a retired teacher passionate about education, established a program to empower seniors through lifelong learning. She organized seminars, lectures, and workshops covering diverse subjects, encouraging seniors to explore new interests and expand their knowledge. This initiative not only stimulated intellectual growth but also fostered a culture of continuous learning among seniors. The enthusiasm of participants spread throughout the community, encouraging others to engage in educational pursuits and demonstrating that age is no barrier to learning.

The Community Outreach Brigade

A group of retired healthcare professionals, led by Dr. Rodriguez, formed a community outreach brigade dedicated to providing medical aid to underserved areas. They organized health camps, provided free check-ups, and offered medical consultations to those in need. Their selfless efforts not only improved access to healthcare but also inspired other seniors to utilize their skills for the betterment of society. The brigade's commitment to serving the community motivated others to volunteer their time and expertise, creating a domino effect of compassionate service.

The Artistic Renaissance

At a retirement home, an art enthusiast named Grace initiated an artistic renaissance. She organized art classes and workshops, encouraging seniors to explore their creative sides through painting, sculpting, and other artistic mediums. The art sessions not only unleashed hidden talents but also provided a therapeutic outlet for self-expression. The vibrant artworks produced by the seniors were showcased in local galleries, drawing attention to their creativity and talent. This initiative sparked a renewed interest in the arts within the community and inspired others to explore their artistic abilities, proving that creativity knows no age boundaries.

In the essence of embracing change and initiating transformative actions, seniors have continually demonstrated the incredible impact of their contributions to communities. Their resilience, wisdom, and passion for instigating positive change have not only enriched their lives but also inspired younger generations to take an active role in shaping a brighter future. As we reflect on these stories of senior-led initiatives, let us not overlook the profound message they impart — that regardless of age, every individual possesses the power to effect change. Seniors serve as guiding beacons, illustrating that a life well-lived is one in which we continually evolve, contribute, and inspire others around us.

The stories of these seniors embarking on remarkable endeavors serve as compelling testaments to the transformative power of ageless determination, resilience, and a compassionate spirit. They remind us that our potential for impact remains ever-present, inviting us to embrace change, step forward with purpose, and contribute positively to our communities. May their journeys serve as an enduring reminder that each one of us possesses the ability to spark change, and by sharing our knowledge, passion, and experiences, we can collectively shape a world of boundless possibilities, leaving a legacy that transcends the passage of time.

Questions to Explore: Taking Action and Changing the World

1. How can the experiences of seniors taking initiative to effect positive change in their communities inspire younger generations to actively participate in community development?

2. What strategies can be adopted to encourage seniors to share their knowledge, skills, and wisdom, fostering a culture of continuous learning and growth within their communities?

3. In what ways can the stories of seniors making transformative impacts influence societal perceptions about the capabilities and contributions of older individuals?

4. How can community leaders and organizations better facilitate opportunities for seniors to lead or participate in initiatives that drive positive change, fostering a more inclusive society?

5. What steps can individuals take to bridge generational divides and create collaborative spaces where seniors and younger generations can collectively work towards common goals, driving positive change in their communities?

CHAPTER SEVEN SUMMARY

In the chapter "Taking Action and Changing the World," seniors take center stage as catalysts for positive change. Through their determination, resilience, and unwavering spirit, they exemplify the transformative power of ageless determination and passion for making a difference. The chapter delves into various stories showcasing seniors who have initiated inspiring initiatives within their communities, breaking stereotypes and illustrating the limitless potential for impact, regardless of age.

It encourages you to view your senior years not as a period of rest, but as an opportunity for continued growth and contribution. The narrative champions the idea that every individual, regardless of age, possesses the ability to instigate positive change. Seniors become the vanguards of change, motivating others to embrace transformation, cultivate resilience, and actively participate in shaping a better world.

Through the stories and reflections within this chapter, the focus remains on the contagious nature of purpose-driven action. It underlines the importance of seniors' roles in driving meaningful changes, inspiring readers to embrace change themselves and become agents of positive transformation within their communities. Ultimately, the chapter serves as a beacon of encouragement, urging individuals of all ages to seize the power within them to effect change and leave an indelible mark on the world.

About The Author

Helen Cummings-Henry *'The Transformation Lady'* is an impassioned advocate for personal growth and transformation, serving as the co-founder and Senior Vice President of Righteous Uplifting Nourishing International, Inc. Her steadfast dedication to effecting change on a person-by-person basis drives her mission to empower individuals, aiding them in discovering their inherent talents and potential.

Navigating the challenges of single parenthood, Helen adeptly raised two sons who have since thrived in reputable corporate careers. Her journey as a mother significantly informs her compassionate approach to nurturing and guiding individuals toward their maximum capabilities.

An accomplished author credited with three books, including her most recent work, "Transforming Lives: Empowering Seniors to Live Their Dreams," Helen's literary pursuits have culminated in the creation of the "Transforming Lives" podcast. This platform provides a conduit for guests to share their transformative narratives, echoing Helen's core objective of influencing lives through the power of storytelling.

Beyond her literary prowess, Helen's diverse talents extend to the theatrical realm. Her one-woman play, "This is my Story," intricately traces her evolution from a reserved girl in Trinidad and Tobago to the empowered woman she embodies today.

Helen's expertise spans coaching, training, and speaking, having acquired certification from Maxwell Leadership. Leveraging these competencies, she mentors and empowers women across various life stages, emphasizing the pivotal significance of personal development and fulfillment.

Demonstrating unwavering dedication, Helen established "Women on the R.U.N. for Jesus," a platform devoted to holistically ministering to women, addressing their spiritual, emotional, and physical well-being based on biblical principles. Her influence has reverberated globally, earning her recognition as a spiritual mentor to women worldwide.

Helen's most recent initiative centers on guiding single women towards self-discovery, enabling them to find fulfillment and prepare for meaningful relationships. Her tireless efforts and unwavering dedication have garnered her numerous accolades, including acknowledgment in Success Magazine's prestigious list of 125 influential individuals, alongside her husband, Tarrent-Arthur Henry. Helen's life and endeavors epitomize her steadfast commitment to empowering others and instigating positive transformations worldwide.

To Contact the Author:

Email: info@helench.org

Website: www.helench.org | www.intlrun.org

Helen's 90-Day Coaching Program

Course Overview:

Discover the Transformation is a meticulously designed 90-day coaching program crafted to facilitate life-altering changes by empowering individuals to take control of their thoughts and behaviors. The curriculum covers essential topics aimed at reducing stress, fostering healthy relationships, combating Imposter Syndrome, and asserting ownership over life. The program's ultimate goal is to equip participants with the skills and confidence necessary for lasting positive changes in both personal and professional spheres.

Key Components:

- Reducing Stress:

- Understanding stress triggers and practical strategies for alleviating stress.

- Implementing mindfulness practices for mental equilibrium.

- Cultivating Healthy Relationships:

- Exploring the foundations of healthy relationships and effective communication.

- Nurturing meaningful connections for mutual growth and support.

- Overcoming Imposter Syndrome:

- Identifying Imposter Syndrome's impact and adopting methods to combat self-doubt.

- Taking Ownership Over Life:

- Cultivating empowerment in decision-making and embracing personal growth.

Course Benefits:

- **Holistic Transformation:** Strategies for personal and professional transformation.

- **Skill Enhancement:** Coping with stress, fostering relationships, and personal growth.

- **Confidence Building:** Navigating life's challenges with assurance.

- **Lasting Change:** Equipping individuals with tools for enduring positive changes.

Helen's 90-Day Coaching Program, Discover the Transformation, is meticulously designed to empower individuals for enduring positive change. Through structured modules, participants embark on a transformative journey toward personal growth and fulfillment.

What Are You Waiting For? Contact – The Transformation Lady – NOW!!!

Contact Helen at www.helench.org to start your journey to a better life.